# UNQUESTIONABLY THE FAMILY CIRCUS

FAWCETT COLUMBINE • NEW YORK

A Fawcett Columbine Book
Published by Ballantine Books

 Published in the United States by Ballantine Books,
a division of Random House, Inc., New York, and simultaneously in
Canada by Random House of Canada Limited, Toronto.

Library of Congress Catalog Card Number: 85-90589

ISBN: 0-449-90147-5

Manufactured in the United States of America

Designed by Gene Siegel

First Edition: September 1985

10 9 8 7 6 5 4 3 2 1

# Questions, questions, questions! Children have always asked questions. And parents have always given the same thoughtful answers.

Nationwide
MOVING
SALE
HOW COME THE PEOPLE NEXT DOOR ARE MOVING, MOMMY?
BIL KEANE

DID YOU GO TO SITTER SCHOOL TO LEARN HOW TO DO THIS?
ALL OF US ARE POTTY TRAINED 'CEPT FOR PJ.
DO YOU KNOW HOW TO MAKE PEANUT-BUTTER FUDGE OR BROWNIES, OR...
IF WE DON'T DO AS YOU SAY ARE YOU GONNA CALL MOMMY AND DADDY AT THE NUMBER THEY GAVE YOU?
THERE'S SOME ICE CREAM IN THE FREEZER-- IF YOU WANT SOME WE'LL HELP YOU EAT IT.
WHAT TV SHOWS ARE WE GOING TO WATCH?
DID YOU BRING THOSE BOOKS TO DO YOUR HOME-WORK OR ARE THEY JUST BE-TEND?
DO YOU LIKE LITTLE KIDS?
ARE YOU ANY GOOD AT READIN' STORIES OUT LOUD?
WILL YOU GET MARRIED SOME DAY?
DID YOU KNOW THAT YOU'RE THE FIFTH SITTER MOMMY PHONED? THE OTHERS WERE ALL BUSY.
YOU DON'T HAFTA BE AFRAID OF BARFY AND SAM. THEY'RE PART OF THE FAMILY.
THE WORST SITTER WE EVER HAD WAS LINDA-- SHE DIDN'T LIKE TO ANSWER QUESTIONS.
GAME
BIL KEANE

WHAT'S THE DIFFERENCE BETWEEN A HOUSE AND A HOME?
I'LL **DRAW** IT FOR YOU.
HOUSE
Wanna play a game with me Grandma?
Dinner's almost ready.
mmm... Smells good hon...
WOOF!
HOME
BIL KEANE

EXCUSE ME, M'AM-- THERE'S A PHONE CALL FOR YOU-- IT'S YOUR BABY SITTER.
JEFFY WON'T GO TO BED WITHOUT SAYING GOOD NIGHT TO YOU... HOLD THE PHONE... I'LL PUT HIM ON...
BIL KEANE

CAN I GET INTO YOUR BAND?
AW, DADDY-- YOU'RE TOO OLD TO PRETEND!
BIL KEANE

MOMMY! I JUST HAD A BAD MOVIE!

YOU'RE NOT TO BUDGE FROM THIS HOUSE TILL YOU'VE FINISHED YOUR HOMEWORK!
AW, MOMMY!
SOMEDAY WHEN YOU GROW UP YOU'LL THANK ME FOR BEING SO STRICT.
MOM, I WANT TO THANK YOU FOR MAKING ME DO MY HOMEWORK BACK IN MARCH OF '82.
BIL KEANE

EVER HAVE A SONG RUNNING AROUND INSIDE YOUR HEAD?
I KEEP HEARING THE SAME TUNE OVER AND OVER.
BEST WAY TO GET RID OF IT IS TO SING IT OUT LOUD.
GOOD IDEA, BRUCE--I'LL GIVE IT A TRY.
OH THE FARMER IN THE DELL...
THE FARMER IN THE DELL...
HEIGH-HO THE DAIRY-OH...
?
BIL KEANE

YOU'RE TO PRACTICE FOR 30 MINUTES.
3 MIN.
4 MIN.
WE HAVE TO GO HOME IN JUST 30 MINUTES!
22 MIN.
23 MIN.
24 MIN.
25 MIN.
26 MIN.
12
BIG

MOMMY, WHAT DOES MY GUARDIAN ANGEL LOOK LIKE?

"Eat your Vegetables!"

Visiting Relative

The Parade

At Church

A Stairway

Scenery From the Back Seat of the Car

COUGH! COUGH!
I HAVE A SORE THROAT.

MILK'S ALL GONE, MOMMY.
THE TELEPHONE WON'T WORK!
MILK

THE JOHN'S BACKED UP.
FLAKES

MORE BAD NEWS FROM WASHINGTON...
The Bulletin
PRICES, TAXES
CONTINUE TO

BIL KEANE

HAVE YOU FINISHED SORTING THOSE PICTURES YET?
NO-- IT MAY TAKE SEVERAL WEEKS.

WHY DOES THE CAR HAVE ITS MOUTH WIDE OPEN, DADDY?
WILL THE TOW TRUCK HAFTA COME LIKE IT DID THE LAST TIME YOU FIXED THE CAR?
MAYBE MOMMY CAN HELP-- SHE'S GOOD AT FIXIN' HER SEWING MACHINE.
WHY DO VOLKSWAGENS KEEP THEIR ENGINES IN THE TRUNK?
WHICH DOES IT TAKE-- "D" BATTERIES OR "C" BATTERIES?
WHICH PART WAS DOIN' ALL THE KNOCKIN', DADDY?
WANT ME TO BLOW THE HORN, DADDY?
SHALL I RUN IN THE HOUSE AND GET YOUR HAMMER AND SAW?
CAN WE LOOK AT THE HORSEPOWERS IN THERE?
BETCHA MOMMY WILL MAKE YOU SCRUB THOSE HANDS BEFORE YOU COME TO THE TABLE.
IF YOU'RE LOOKIN' FOR THE GAS TANK, DADDY, IT'S IN THE BACK.
BIL KEANE

BILLY! MOMMY'S WAITING TO SEE YOUR REPORT CARD.

BILLY AND DOLLY TEAM UP WITH HER VERSION OF THE EASTER BUNNY AND HIS ART.
S. Claus
E. Bunny
The Easter Bunny lives at the North Pole next door to Santa Claus.
OK, Guys, More Chocolate!
He has lots of help from his little rabbit elves.
He grows Jelly beans on his big Jelly Bean Farm.
The Jelly Beans get ripe just before Easter.
On Easter Eve the Bunny travels around the world in his Volkswagen Rabbit.
He hides the eggs in easy-to-find places for good boys and girls and hard-to-find places for the baddies.
Happy Easter!
Then he goes out for an Easter Brunch of Egg nog and ham.

BIL KEANE

Blessed are the peacemakers....

A GOOD
STUDENT
IS CLEAN
AND NEAT
BIL
KEANE

HAPPY MOTHER'S DAY!
I MADE THIS CAKE FOR YOU, MOMMY. DADDY HELPED A LITTLE.
I PICKED THESE MYSELF!
My MOMmy
I LOVE YOU
x XXX

ENJOY THEM EVERY MINUTE, DEARY. BEFORE YOU CAN TURN AROUND THEY'LL BE GROWN.
I TOLD THE PRINCIPAL YOU WANTED TO BE PRESIDENT OF PTA. IS THAT OKAY?
WHEN YOU READ MY HORRORSCOPE, WHY DOES IT ALWAYS SAY 'AND BE A GOOD BOY TODAY'?
HERE'S A VERY 'PORTANT PAPER YOU'RE SUPPOSED TO FILL OUT FOR SCHOOL, MOMMY.
STOP THAT WASTIN', JEFFY! DON'T YOU KNOW THERE'S AN OIL SHORTAGE?
WHY DIDN'T YOU THINK OF THAT BEFORE I DRESSED YOU?
WE ARE IN BED!
BIL KEANE

FALL
I'M PUTTING THESE TULIPS TO BED SO THEY CAN SLEEP FOR THE WINTER.

WINTER
Z Z
Z Z
Z Z
Z Z Z

SPRING
MOMMY! THE TULIPS ARE AWAKE!

MOMMY! MOMMY!
COME QUICK!
WHAT TOOK YOU SO LONG?

PLAYGROUND
RULES
NOW CAN WE GO HOME AND WATCH TV?
BIL KEANE

ARE YOU SURE DOCTOR CUTHBERTSON KNOWS WE'RE HERE, MOMMY? HE DIDN'T COME OUT TO SAY HELLO.
I HOPE WE DON'T GET ANY SHOTS 'CAUSE I MIGHT HAFTA CRY AND YELL AND KICK AND...
DO DOCTORS EVER GET SICK LIKE REAL PEOPLE DO?
GRANDMA SAYS WHEN SHE WAS LITTLE THE DOCTOR CAME TO HER HOUSE. IS SHE JUST KIDDING US, MOMMY?
ARE ALL THESE OTHER PEOPLE SICK, MOMMY OR JUST HERE FOR CHECK-UPS, TOO?
KNOW WHAT, MOMMY? THAT MUSIC SOUNDS 'ZACTLY LIKE THE KIND WE HEAR IN ELEVATORS.
IS THIS THE SAME DOCTOR WE TAKE FROM FOR BABIES?
PLEASE SIGN IN
SHALL I READ THIS COMIC BOOK OUT LOUD SO EVERYBODY CAN HEAR IT?
HOW COME THERE ARE ALWAYS SO MANY GOLF MAGAZINES HERE?
THE SATURDAY EVENING POST
1918
GOLF
Collier's
WOW! THAT LADY HAS A FAT TUMMY, DOESN'T SHE, MOMMY?
WHY DO YOU KEEP SAYIN' "SHHH," MOMMY? IS SOMEBODY SLEEPING?

...AND THE GENIE SAID TO ALADDIN, "HOW MAY I SERVE YOU, MASTER?"
ALADDIN

BIL KEANE

MMMM! IT'S GOOD! TASTES LIKE CANDY!
HERE COMES THE AIRPLANE IN FOR A LANDING!
DON'T YOU WANT TO BELONG TO THE CLEAN PLATE CLUB?
HERE COMES THE CHOO-CHOO, PJ-- OPEN UP AND LET IT IN.
IT'LL MAKE YOU GROW BIG AND STRONG LIKE DADDY.
DO YOU KNOW ANY NEW TRICKS, MOMMY? NONE OF THE OLD ONES WORKED.
Bil Keane

WE'LL HANDLE THIS EXACTLY AS IT'S WORDED IN THE CONTRACT! I'LL HAVE NOTHING FURTHER TO SAY. UNDERSTAND? OKAY.
BYE-BYE.
BYE-BYE?
C
BIL KEANE

DOLLY ALWAYS GETS MORE ICE CREAM THAN I DO.
NO I DON'T! JEFFY OR BILLY ALWAYS GETS THE MOST!
UH-UH! MINE IS ALWAYS THE LITTLEST.
THERE'S ONE WAY TO SETTLE THIS.
ICE CREAM
POSTAL SCALES
BIL KEANE

TODAY'S CHILDREN HAVE EVERYTHING SPELLED OUT FOR THEM. THEY JUST DON'T LEARN TO USE THEIR IMAGINATION.
LOOK! I CLIMBED TO THE TOP OF MOUNT EVEREST!
IN ONE LEAP I CROSS THE OCEAN TO AUSTRALIA.
THERE'S A GIANT KANGAROO!
WOW! A BURIED TREASURE WORTH FIFTY MILLION DOLLARS!
PANETELAS
STRIKE THREE! ANOTHER PERFECT GAME FOR THE GREATEST PITCHER EVER!
HERE'S THE WORLD'S BEST BULL FIGHTER FACING A FEROCIOUS BULL!
NOW, FANS, I'LL DO MY LATEST HIT, THE TOP-SELLING RECORD IN THE COUNTRY...
BIL KEANE

I HOPE AND PRAY OUR CHILDREN WILL NEVER HAVE TO GO TO WAR!
BEEP!
BOOP!
BEEP!
3170
3
PKEW!
BOOP!
BEEP!
PKEW!
BOOP!

THE CIRCUS WAS ON TV.
POP CORN

I FELL OUT OF BED!

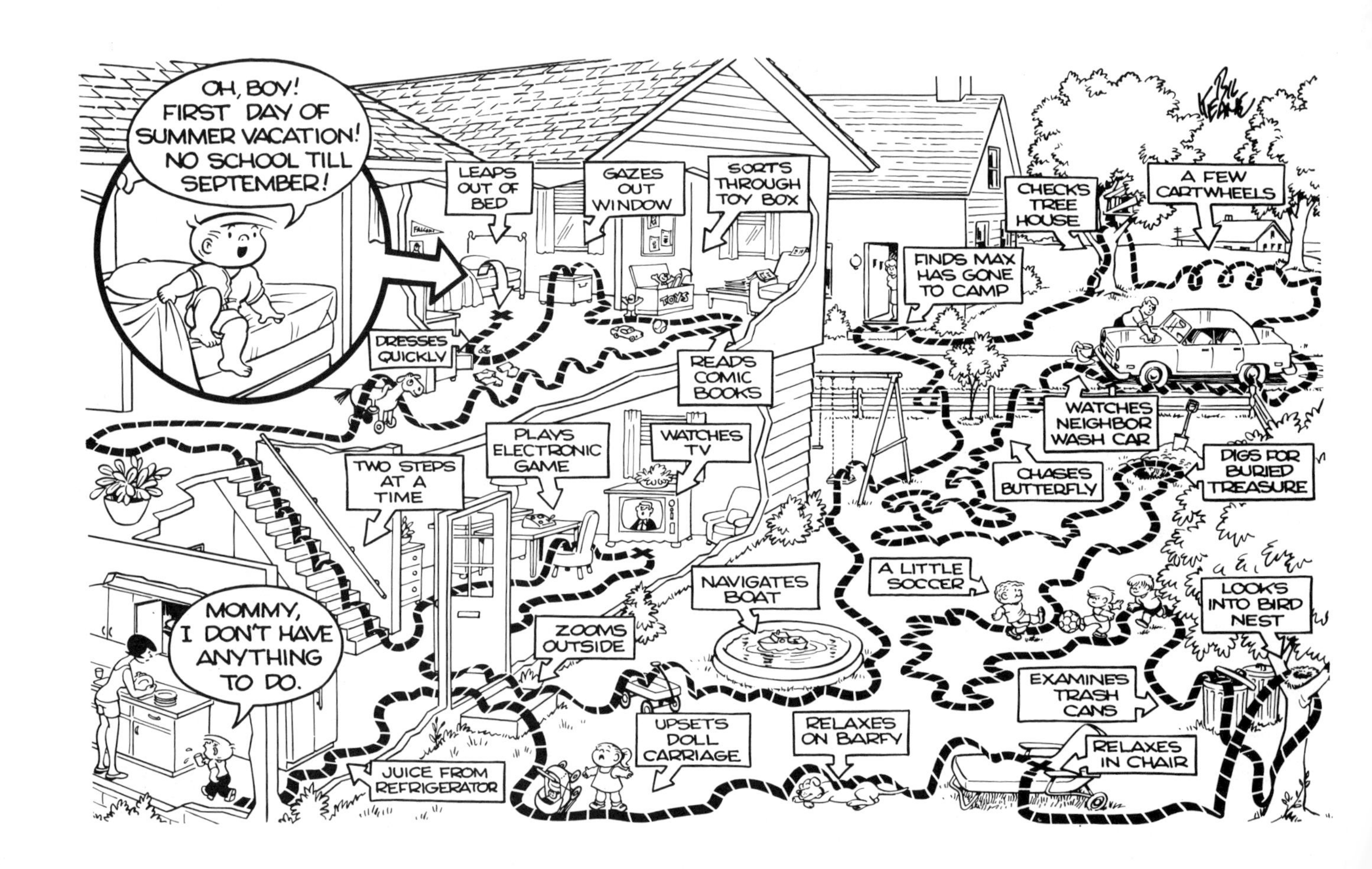
OH, BOY! FIRST DAY OF SUMMER VACATION! NO SCHOOL TILL SEPTEMBER!
LEAPS OUT OF BED
FALCONS
DRESSES QUICKLY
GAZES OUT WINDOW
SORTS THROUGH TOY BOX
TOYS
READS COMIC BOOKS
TWO STEPS AT A TIME
PLAYS ELECTRONIC GAME
WATCHES TV
ZOOMS OUTSIDE
NAVIGATES BOAT
FINDS MAX HAS GONE TO CAMP
CHECKS TREE HOUSE
A FEW CARTWHEELS
WATCHES NEIGHBOR WASH CAR
CHASES BUTTERFLY
DIGS FOR BURIED TREASURE
A LITTLE SOCCER
LOOKS INTO BIRD NEST
EXAMINES TRASH CANS
RELAXES IN CHAIR
RELAXES ON BARFY
UPSETS DOLL CARRIAGE
JUICE FROM REFRIGERATOR
MOMMY, I DON'T HAVE ANYTHING TO DO.

JEFFY! ARE YOU BEING A GOOD BOY?
YES, MOMMY!

HEY, BILLY! THIS IS A **NEAT** PARTY!
YEAH-- IT'S A LOT BETTER THAN JUST A COOKOUT IN THE BACK YARD.
H
SUNNY
76
FAIR
WHO WANTS TO PLAY "KING OF THE MOUNTAIN"?
GUESS WE LUCKED OUT WITH THIS RAIN.
THERE GOES YOUR PLASTIC PLANTS MOMMY!
I'LL PUT THESE PLANTS OUT IN THE RAIN FOR A DRINK.
Family Album
IT'S RAININ' HERE, TOO, MOM, BUT WE'RE HAVIN' IT INSIDE.
THESE POTATO CHIPS ARE SOGGY.
I LIKE MINE RARE WITH CHEESE.
WE'RE SWIMMING IN THE BATH-TUB! IS THAT OKAY?
TATO CHIPS
BIL KEANE

BILLY, WOULD YOU RUN DOWN TO THE BASEMENT AND GET A HAMMER FOR ME?
AND BE CAREFUL--THE LIGHT IS BURNED OUT.
BIL KEANE

OH, THEY'RE NO BOTHER. I JUST KEEP REMINDING MYSELF OF THE $38 AN HOUR I CHARGE.
HORACE THE PLUMBER
CALKING

I'LL BETCHA WE'RE THE VERY FIRST DAD AND SON WHO EVER WENT FISHIN' IN THIS SPOT.
BIL KEANE

HAPPY FATHER'S DAY!
Another page contributed by seven year-old Billy.
This is my Favorite Music!
Brummmm
Daddy driving into the garage
The frogs and crickets at night.
Kittycat's purring because it means she's happy.
PJ playing in his crib in the morning.
clink
Mommy getting the dishes out for dinner.
People laughing downstairs when we have company.
The quiet when it's snowing.
Voooomm
The lawn mower means it is Saturday and Daddy's home.

DADDY'S WEARING THE TIE I GAVE HIM!
THAT'S NOT THE SHIRT I GAVE YOU, DADDY!
LET'S SEE YOUR UNDER-WEAR.
THOSE AREN'T MY SOCKS--AND WHERE'S THE SWEATER PJ GAVE YOU?
BIL KEANE

MOMMY, WILL YOU TIE MY SHOE FOR ME?
BIL KEANE

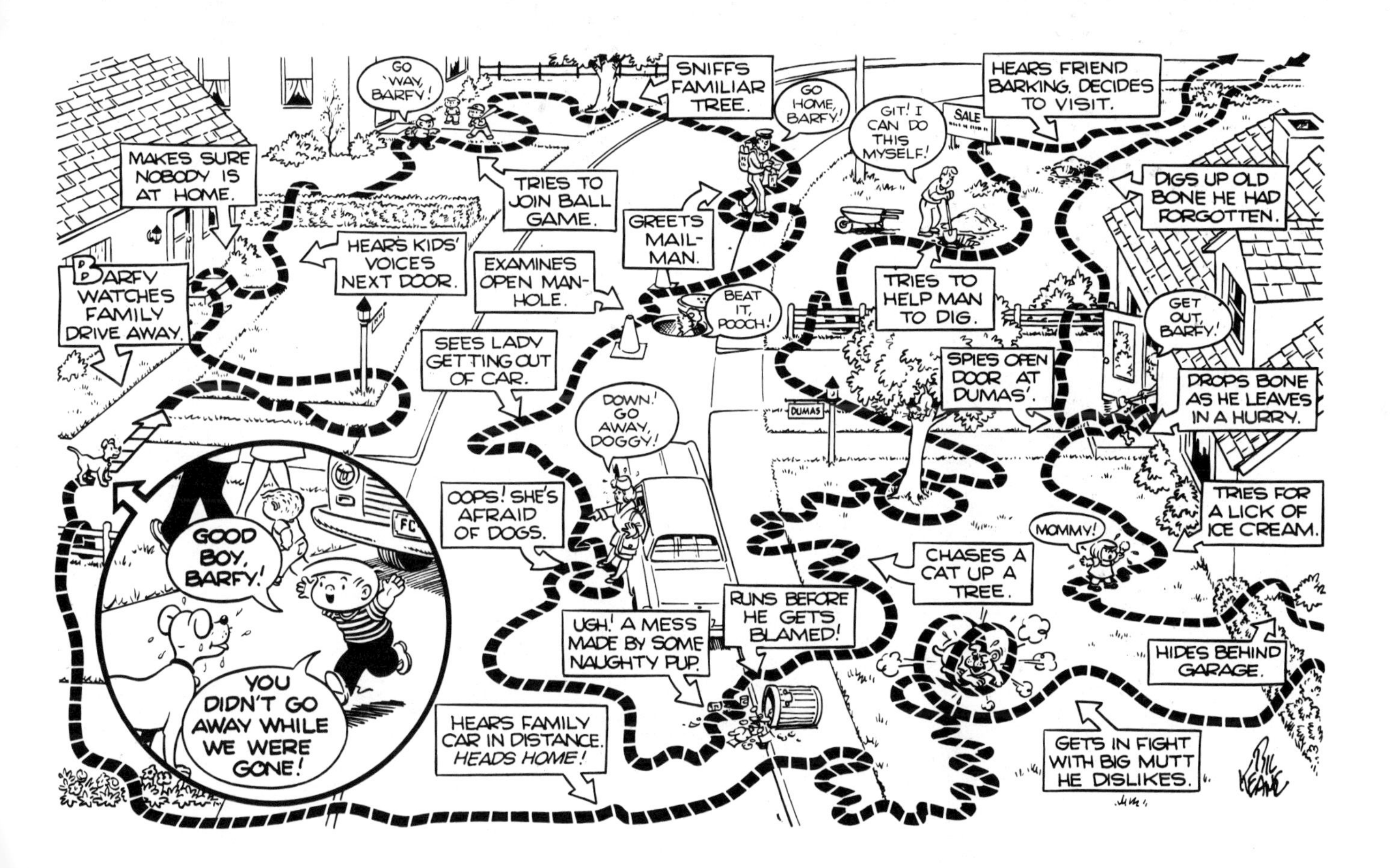
BARFY WATCHES FAMILY DRIVE AWAY.
MAKES SURE NOBODY IS AT HOME.
HEARS KIDS' VOICES NEXT DOOR.
TRIES TO JOIN BALL GAME.
GO 'WAY, BARFY!
SNIFFS FAMILIAR TREE.
GREETS MAIL-MAN.
GO HOME, BARFY!
EXAMINES OPEN MAN-HOLE.
BEAT IT, POOCH!
SEES LADY GETTING OUT OF CAR.
DOWN! GO AWAY, DOGGY!
OOPS! SHE'S AFRAID OF DOGS.
TRIES TO HELP MAN TO DIG.
GIT! I CAN DO THIS MYSELF!
SALE
HEARS FRIEND BARKING, DECIDES TO VISIT.
DIGS UP OLD BONE HE HAD FORGOTTEN.
SPIES OPEN DOOR AT DUMAS'.
DUMAS
GET OUT, BARFY!
DROPS BONE AS HE LEAVES IN A HURRY.
TRIES FOR A LICK OF ICE CREAM.
MOMMY!
CHASES A CAT UP A TREE.
HIDES BEHIND GARAGE.
GETS IN FIGHT WITH BIG MUTT HE DISLIKES.
RUNS BEFORE HE GETS BLAMED!
UGH! A MESS MADE BY SOME NAUGHTY PUP.
HEARS FAMILY CAR IN DISTANCE. HEADS HOME!
GOOD BOY, BARFY!
YOU DIDN'T GO AWAY WHILE WE WERE GONE!
BIL KEANE

The INTERPRETER
DAP FWEEP.
HE'S SAYING OUR DADDY IS TAKING A NAP.
VRUM TAT.
HE SAYS BARFY'S CHASING A CAT.
FWACK FWACK!
HE WANTS YOU TO PLAY HIS "GOIN' QUACKERS" RECORD.
Neal's Music
UM MAME TOOKS.
HE'S TELLIN' YOU MOMMY IS BAKIN' COOKIES, GRANDMA.
PJ IS LEARNIN' TO TALK REAL GOOD.
FRMLCH.
BESS QRRL?
HE'D LIKE YOU TO DRESS HIM.
Bil Keane

BIL KEANE
LOOK, DADDY!
LOOK AT ME, DADDY!
DADDY! WATCH WHAT I CAN DO!
LOOK HERE, DADDY!
OVER HERE! WATCHIN', DADDY?
HEY, DADDY! LOOK AT THIS!
LOOK AT ME!
WATCH THIS, DADDY!
WANNA SEE SOME-THING NEAT, DADDY? WATCH!

BRUMMM RUMMM!
OUT YOU GO, PJ-- DADDY'S READY TO LEAVE.
RADIO BLARING
SOME-BODY'S BEEN SITTING IN MY SEAT!
WIPERS FLIPPING
STICKY STEERING WHEEL
TURN SIGNALS BLINKING
BIL KEANE

WANNA HEAR A JOKE?
WHAT DOES THE BRIGHTEST, BEST LOOKIN' KID IN THE WORLD HAVE FOR BREAKFAST?
I DON'T KNOW. WHAT?
WELL, THIS MORNING I HAD JUICE, CEREAL...
WANNA HEAR A JOKE, DADDY?
SURE.
WHAT DOES THE BESTEST LOOKING, BRIGHTEST GUY IN THE WORLD EAT FOR HIS BREAKFAST? GIVE UP?
YES.
BILLY HAD SOME CEREAL AND JUICE THIS MORNING.
BIL KEANE

WHO GOT ALL THESE OUT?
NOT ME.
NOT ME!
WHO TOOK MY RADIO BATTERIES?
NOT ME.
NOT ME.
WHO ATE UP ALL THE PUDDING?
NOT ME!
WHO WROTE ON THIS WALL?
NOT ME.
WHO DID THIS TO MY BRAND NEW MAGAZINE?
NOT ME.
NOT ME.
NOT ME.
SOMEWHERE IN THIS HOUSE IS AN INVISIBLE GREMLIN NAMED "NOT ME."
I BELIEVE YOU'RE RIGHT.
BIL KEANE
...THEN AFTER THAT I GRABBED SOME BATTERIES, PIGGED OUT ON SOME PUDDING,...
...SCRIBBLED ON THE WALL, AND CUT UP A MAGAZINE... WHEW! WHAT A DAY!
NOT ME

WHEN IS THE RAIN GONNA STOP, DADDY?
I'M TIRED OF READING AND COLORING AND PLAYIN' GAMES, DADDY-- WHAT ELSE CAN WE DO?
WHY CAN'T WE THROW THE FRISBEE INSIDE, MOMMY?
THAT BOAT OUT THERE MUST BE WATERPROOF ON THE BOTTOM AND THE TOP.
WHY CAN'T WE GO DOWN TO THE BEACH ANYWAY? WE CAN WEAR OUR BATHIN' SUITS.
MY BUCKET AND SHOVEL ARE STILL ALMOST BRAND NEW.
IF WE WERE HOME SOME OF THE GUYS WOULD COME OVER TO PLAY IN MY ROOM.
ONE GOOD THING-- NOBODY'S GETTIN' SUN-BURNED.
I'LL BET THE FISHES LIKE THIS WEATHER 'CAUSE THERE'S NOBODY OUT THERE CATCHIN' THEM.
YOU DIDN'T WASH THE CAR, DID YOU, DADDY? THAT'S WHAT USUALLY MAKES IT RAIN.
TELL BILLY TO STOP WALKIN' AROUND SINGING "RAINDROPS KEEP FALLING ON MY HEAD."
DO WE HAFTA PAY FOR THIS PLACE EVEN WHEN IT'S RAINING?
BLUE LAGOON
THE DAILY PILOT
MORE RAIN FORECAST FOR THE WEEK
52
COLORING BOOK
BIL KEANE

BILLY HITS THE BEACH
NO PARKING
CHASES GULLS
PLAYS WITH FRIENDLY DOG. (DOG GETS TIRED)
DIGS PART WAY TO CHINA
Billy the Great
PRINTS NAME IN SAND
BUILDS ELABORATE CASTLE
COLLECTS PILE OF SEASHELLS
BRIEFLY JOINS JOGGER
READS GRAFITTI ON PILING
CHECKS PIER FISHERMEN
GETS INTO VOLLEY BALL GAME
SHOWS KID HOW TO TOSS FRISBEE
FRISBEE
LISTENS TO MUSIC
ASKS FOR FREE SAMPLES
ICE CREAM
JOINS BALL GAME
TIME TO GO, BILLY.
BUT I HAVEN'T GONE IN THE WATER YET.
CHECKS OUT OLD BOAT
Bil Keane

YOU LOOK GREAT! NOW DON'T MOVE WHILE I GET THE CAMERA SET.
F:8 OR 5.6
SHUTTER SPEED: 125
ASA 100
6 FEET...

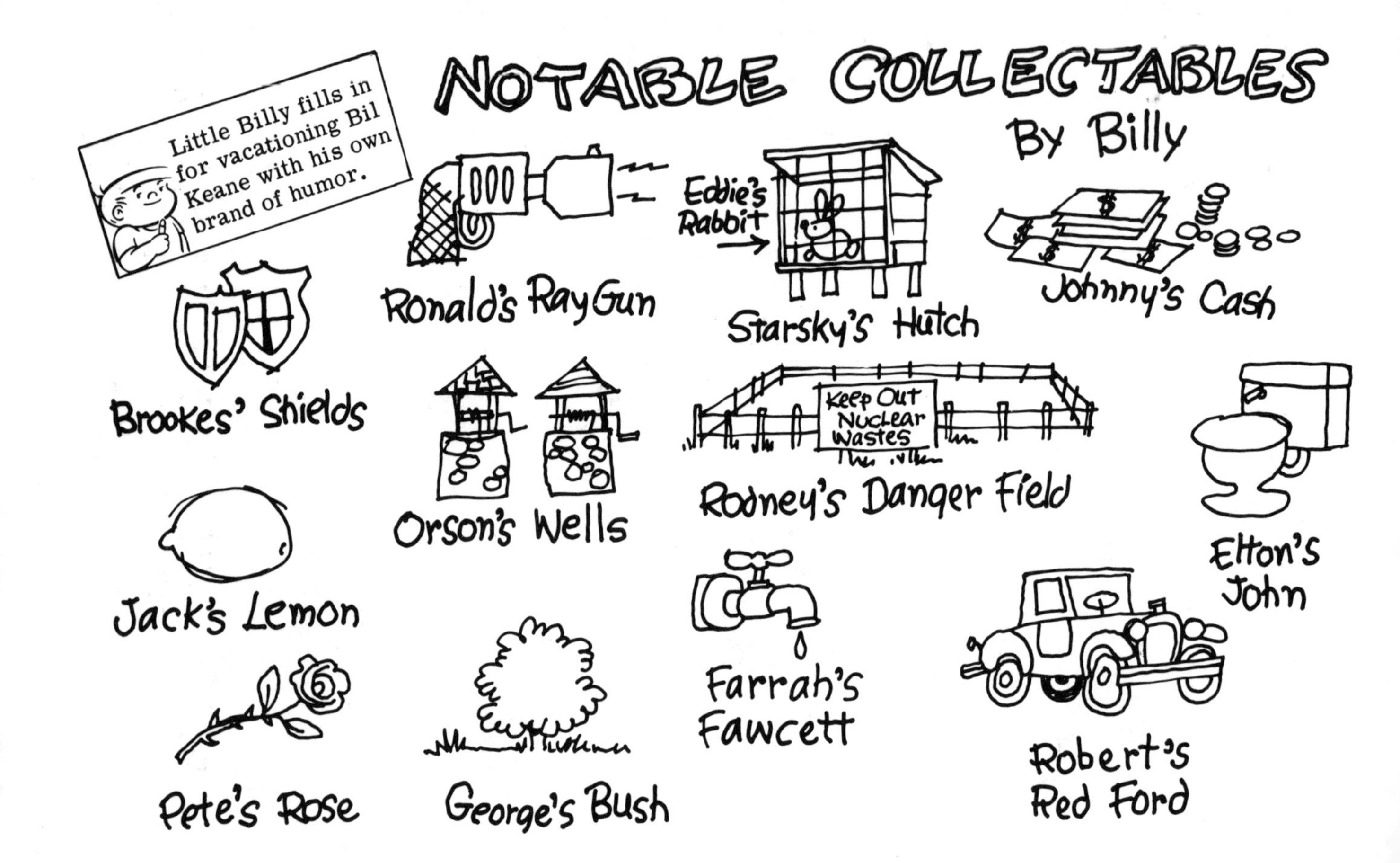
NOTABLE COLLECTABLES
By Billy
Little Billy fills in for vacationing Bil Keane with his own brand of humor.
Ronald's RayGun
Eddie's Rabbit
Starsky's Hutch
Johnny's Cash
Brookes' Shields
Orson's Wells
Keep Out Nuclear Wastes
Rodney's Danger Field
Elton's John
Jack's Lemon
Farrah's Fawcett
Robert's Red Ford
Pete's Rose
George's Bush

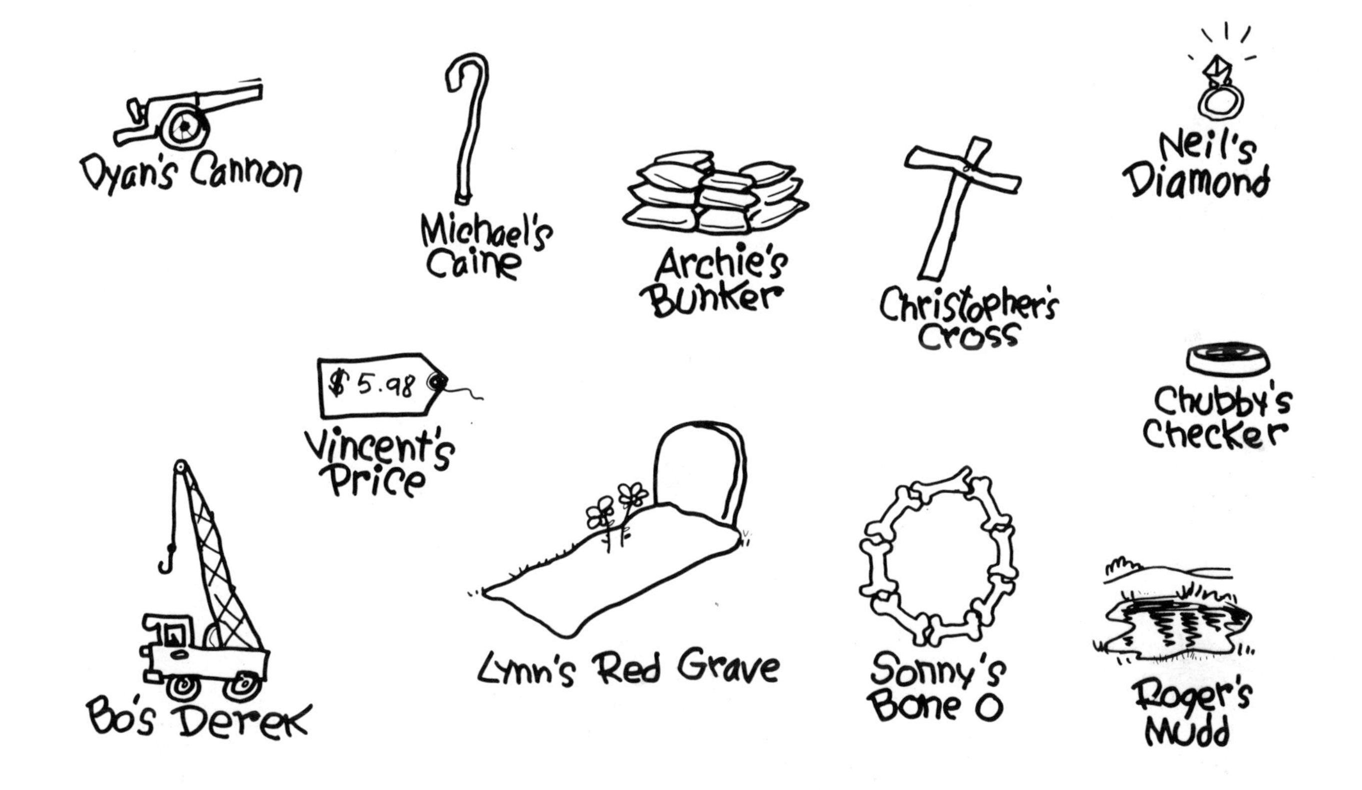
Dyan's Cannon
Michael's Caine
Archie's Bunker
Christopher's Cross
Neil's Diamond
$ 5.98
Vincent's Price
Chubby's Checker
Bo's Derek
Lynn's Red Grave
Sonny's Bone O
Roger's Mudd

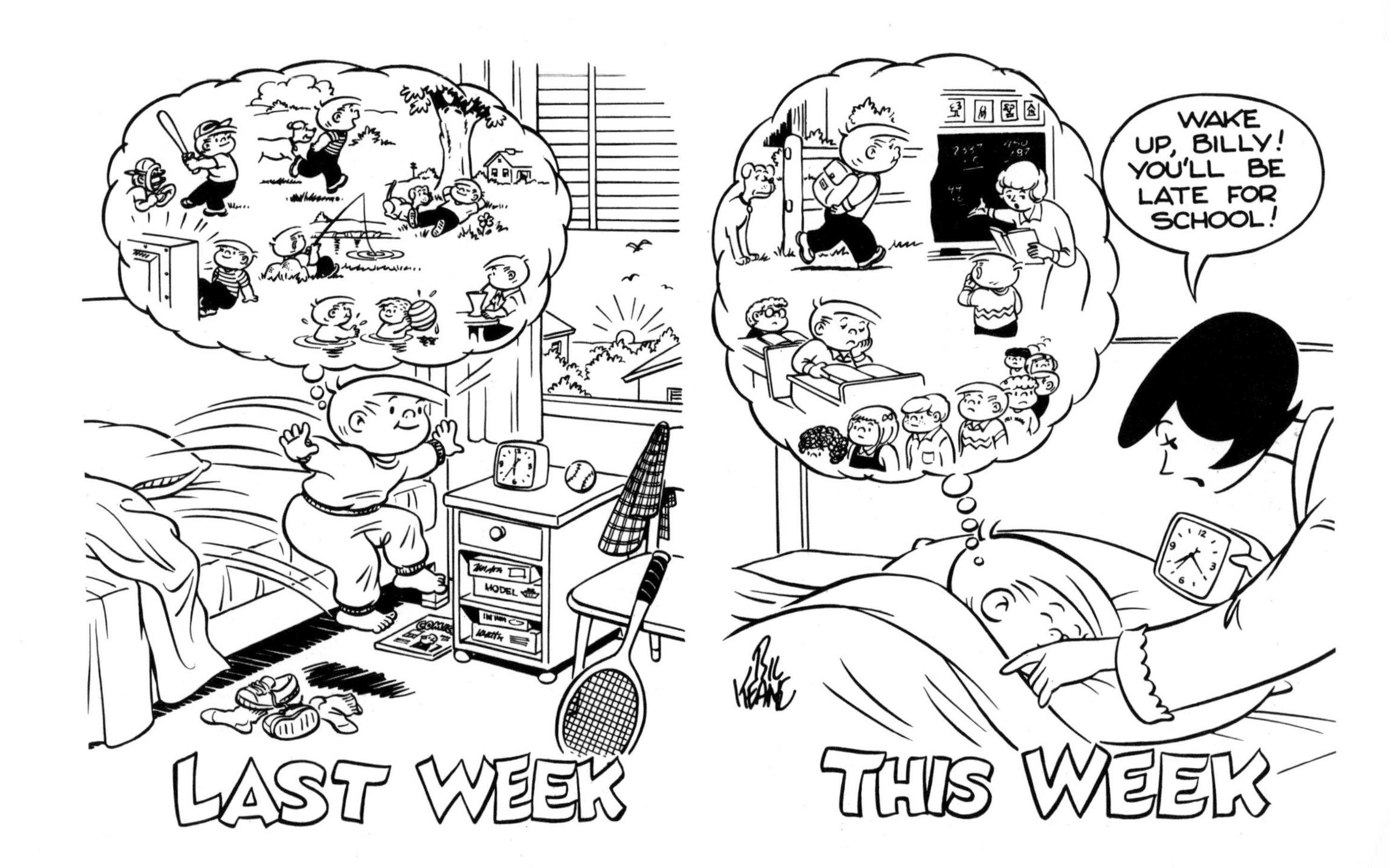

HOBBY
MODEL
COMICS
WAKE UP, BILLY! YOU'LL BE LATE FOR SCHOOL!
BIL KEANE
LAST WEEK
THIS WEEK

MOMMY! JEFFY PUSHED MY DOLL HOUSE OVER!
SHAME ON YOU! STOP BEING MEAN TO YOUR BIG SISTER.
YOU'RE VERY NAUGHTY. UNDERSTAND?
JEFFY?
DON'T CRY, HONEY...
THERE, THERE... DID MOMMY MAKE JEFFY CRY? AWW...
PAT PAT
BIL KEANE

BACK-TO-SCHOOL TIME MEANS HALLOWEEN IS RIGHT AROUND THE CORNER! THEN THANKSGIVING, AND CHRISTMAS... THEN...
SCHOOL ZONE
TRICK OR TREAT
BIL KEANE

THEL! THE DOOR MAT ISN'T FOR SALE, IS IT?
WELCOME
DOWN, BOY! I PAID FOR THIS!
DIDN'T YOU SAY THAT OL' TV SET HAS ABOUT HAD IT, DADDY?
I'VE CHANGED MY MIND ABOUT SELLING THIS GOOD OL' ROD AND REEL.
RECORD ALBUMS
LET'S GO INSIDE-- I'LL SELL YA SOME STUFF FROM THE 'FRIGERATOR.
MINE!
MOMMY WILL LOWER THE PRICE IF YOU HAGGLE.
GARAGE SALE TODAY
BIL KEANE

GEE, MOMMY, YOU AND DADDY WOULD NEVER SELL THIS HOUSE, WOULD YOU?
I DON'T REALLY THINK WE EVER COULD, BILLY.
TOY
BIL KEANE

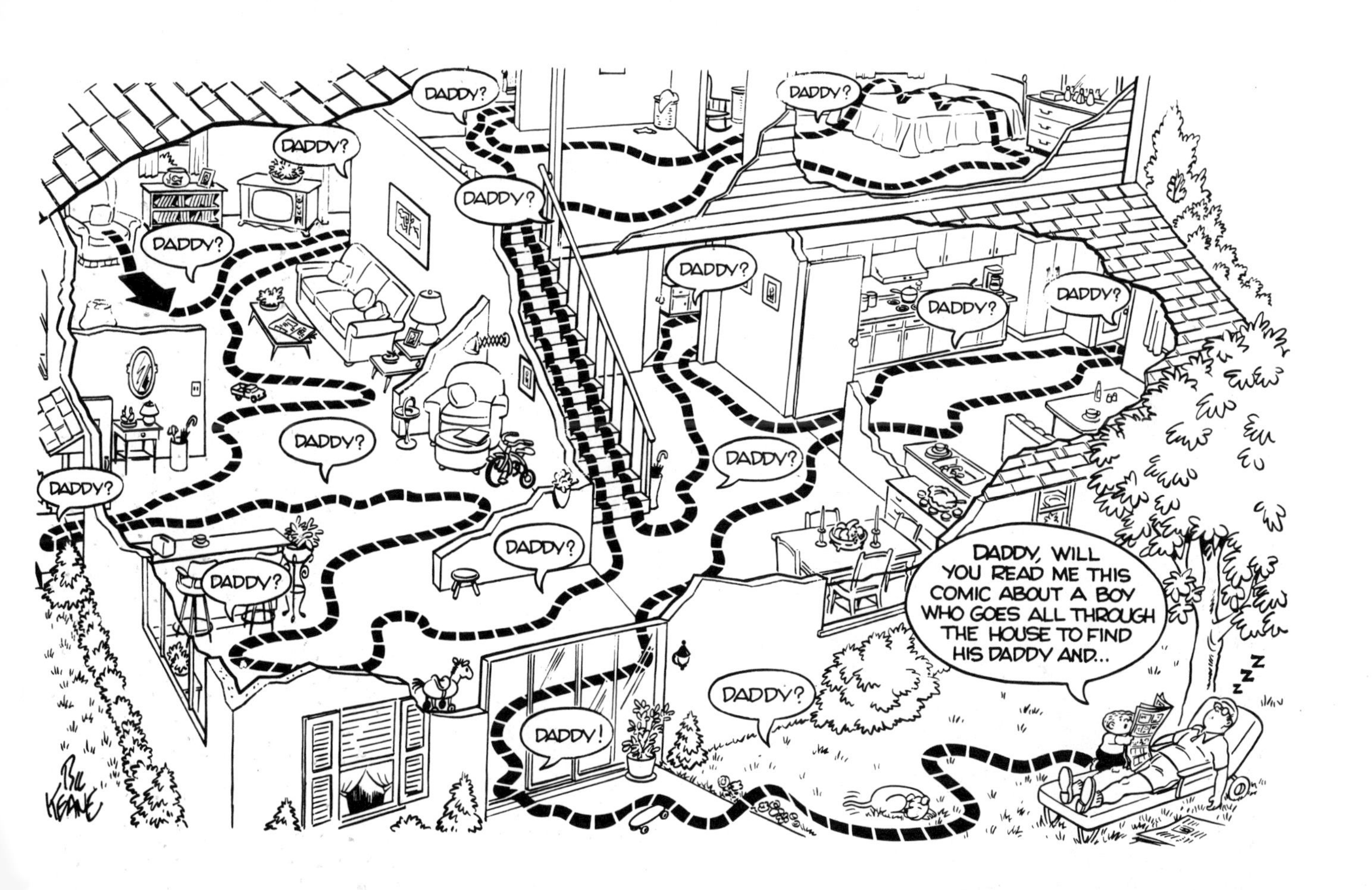

DADDY?
DADDY?
DADDY?
DADDY?
DADDY?
DADDY?
DADDY?
DADDY?
DADDY?
DADDY?
DADDY?
DADDY?
DADDY?
DADDY!
DADDY?
DADDY, WILL YOU READ ME THIS COMIC ABOUT A BOY WHO GOES ALL THROUGH THE HOUSE TO FIND HIS DADDY AND...
Z Z Z
BIL KEANE

HI, MOMMY! WE'RE PLAYING BARBER.
EMERGENCY!
Bob's
BIL KEANE

WE GO OVER TO SCHOOL, DOWN TO GRANDMA'S, UP TO THE STORE, OUT TO THE FARM IN TO TOWN...
SCHOOL
Grandma's
STORE
FARM
TOWN
BIL KEANE

WHEN WILL THERE EVER BE SOME PEACE AND QUIET AROUND THIS HOUSE?
TICK
TOCK
TICK
TOCK
Grandpa
52
BIL KEANE

GOOD NIGHT, JEFFY-- SLEEP TIGHT. PLEASANT DREAMS.

BIL KEANE

YOU'RE NOT MADE OF SUGAR--YOU WON'T MELT.
PICK UP THE TOWEL. IT'S NOT GOING TO BITE YOU!
IT'S JUST A BREEZE. YOU'RE NOT GOING TO BLOW AWAY.

Daddy's Birthday
By Billy
Happy Birthday to you... Happy...
?
We all sang to the cake
TENNIS
I hope these will make me play better Tennis
So do I.
Mommy gave Daddy the usual present—clothes!
My favorite!
I picked it out and Mommy paid for it.
Can I smell it?
Dolly gave him some after shave lotion
Just what I wanted!
Mommy picked it out.
Jeffy gave him a book
They're the color I like best
Mommy picked those out too.
PJ gave him PJ's.
Grandma gave him a phone call
PJ cried because he didn't get any presents

COOKIES
BIL KEANE

FRONT SEAT!
FRONT SEAT!
I SAID IT FIRST! I SIT IN FRONT!
NO! ME! I GET IT!
NO YOU DON'T!
MINE!
FC - 1
BIL KEANE

BILLY IS OUR TOP STUDENT.
Billy: Straight A's
ALL RIGHT, HEREAFTER WE'LL LINE UP ACCORDING TO SIZE--SMALLEST FIRST. BILLY, YOU'RE THE LEADER.
I'M **FIRST** IN MY CLASS! MISS McELFRESH SAYS I'M THE **LEADER**!
WONDERFUL, BILLY! I'M SO PROUD OF YOU.
BIL KEANE

DO WE HAFTA WAIT TILL WE GET HOME TO CARVE IT?
THIS IS JUST LIKE PICKIN' OUT A CHRISTMAS TREE, ONLY IT'S NOT AS COLD.
WE'VE BEEN DRAWING PUMPKINS AT SCHOOL, BUT THEY SURE DO LOOK DIFFERENT IN PERSON.
THAT ONE'S NO GOOD, DADDY. IT HAS A DENT IN ONE OF ITS CHEEKS.
CAN WE GET ONE FOR EACH OF US?
LET'S NOT GET THE ONE BILLY'S SITTIN' ON!
HOW COULD PETER, PETER PUMPKIN EATER PUT HIS WIFE INTO ONE OF THESE?
IT'S A LUCKY THING PUMPKINS ARE ORANGE--THEY TIE IN WITH THE FALL COLORS.
HOW MANY PUMPKINS DO YOU NEED TO MAKE A PIE, MOMMY?
WHAT KIND OF A FACE WILL HE HAVE--MAD OR GLAD?
NEXT WE HAVE TO FIGURE OUT WHAT WE'RE GONNA DRESS UP AS ON HALLOWEEN.
APPLE CIDER
CORN
BIL KEANE

MOMMY? YOU TOLD ME TO LET YOU KNOW IF THE POT ON THE KITCHEN STOVE BOILED OVER. WELL, IT BOILED OVER.

OH, MY! IT'S DARTH VADER! AND A WICKED WITCH! AND A SCARY GHOST!
AND LOOK AT THE FUNNY CLOWN.
I'M FRIGHTENED!
I'LL NEVER GUESS WHO THESE STRANGERS ARE!
TRICK OR TREAT
TRICK OR TREAT
AW, C'MON, GRANDMA-- IT'S **US**!
TRICK OR TREAT!
WE FOOLED YOU, GRANDMA!
TRICK OR TREAT
TRICK OR TREAT

I'D SURE LIKE TO GET MY HANDS ON THE DEAR NEIGHBORHOOD KIDS WHO SOAPED UP OUR CAR WINDOWS.
WHEN I WAS LITTLE WE HAD "MISCHIEF NIGHT" AND WE WOULD...
NOBODY IS TO EAT ANY OF THAT TRICK OR TREAT STUFF 'TIL AFTER BREAKFAST.
WE GOT THE GUM FROM THE ROTHS, COOKIES FROM THE KUBERTS, THE CANDY BAR FROM THE WOLFES, THE EVERS ONLY GAVE APPLES...
WHILE YOU'RE UP THERE PUTTING AWAY THE HALLOWEEN THINGS, MOMMY, HOW 'BOUT GETTING OUT THE CHRISTMAS DECORATIONS?
...THE MONEY IS FROM GRANDMA...
DOGGY TREATS
TRICK OR TREAT
TRICK OR TREAT
BIL KEANE

KITTYCAT WON'T COME OUT FROM UNDER THE BED.
EASY. LET'S GO TO THE KITCHEN.
WHAT ARE YOU GONNA DO WITH THE CAN OPENER?
RRRRRNNNNNNNNNN
SEAFOOD DINNER

LET'S GO, JEFFY! COME OUT OF THERE-- IT'S TIME FOR BED.
AGHHH! YOU SAW ME! I WAS HIDIN' JUST LIKE E.T.!

* CONTRACT
MEMOS
Fall Meeting
MONDAY
TUES
HI, DADDY!

SMELLS GOOD! WHAT IS IT?
IT'S CALLED "I DUNNO."
WHY WOULD YOU CALL A DELICIOUS CASSEROLE "I DUNNO?"
YOU'LL SEE.
WHAT WOULD EVERYBODY LIKE FOR DINNER?
BIL KEANE
I DUNNO.
YOU GOT IT!

IT WAS THE LOUDEST NOISE EVER HEARD ANYWHERE...
ROCK
SCHOOL

NO.
NO!
DO YOU REALLY MEAN THAT?
YES!
MOMMY SAID YES.
BIL KEANE

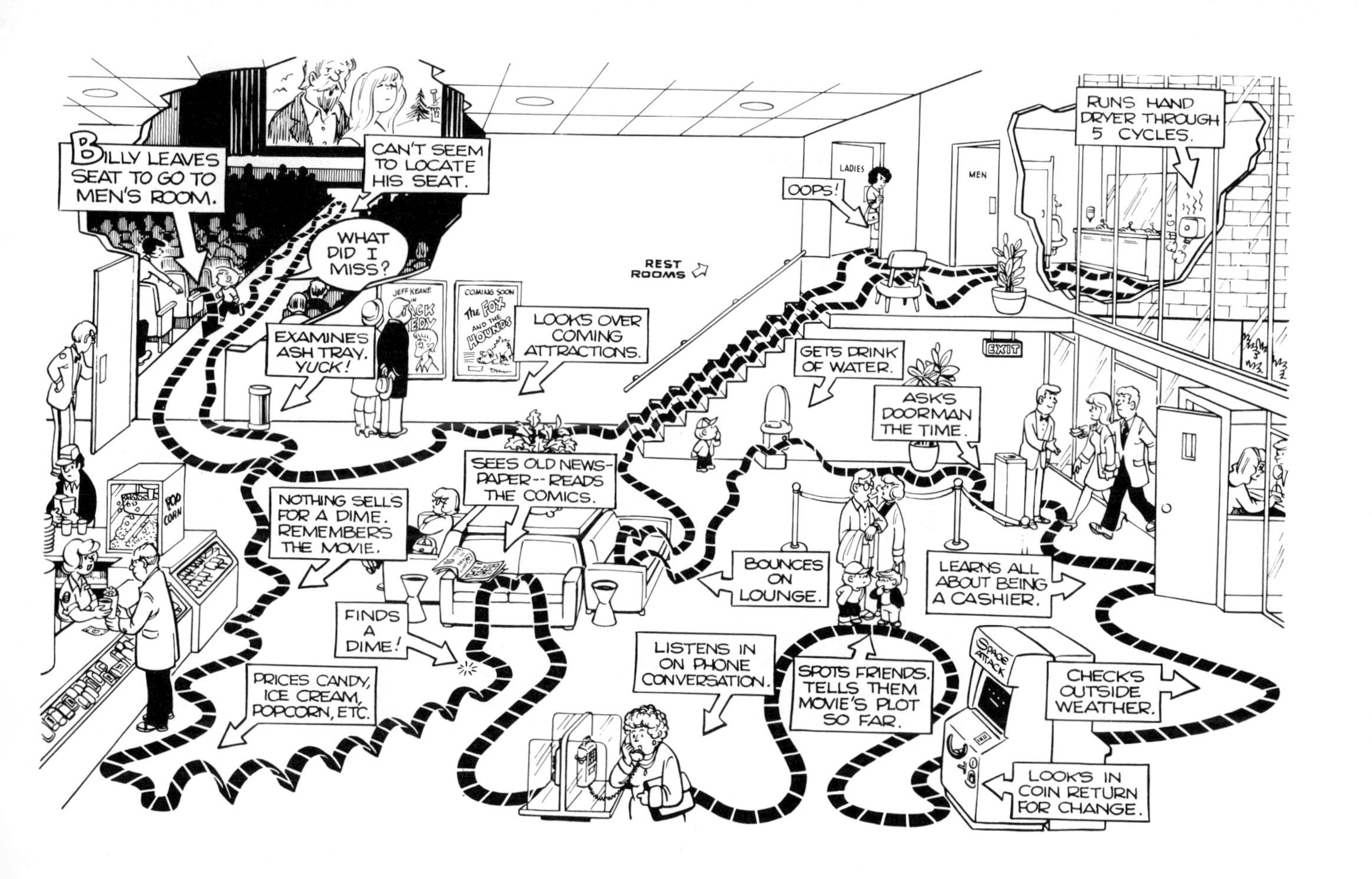

BILLY LEAVES SEAT TO GO TO MEN'S ROOM.
CAN'T SEEM TO LOCATE HIS SEAT.
WHAT DID I MISS?
EXAMINES ASH TRAY. YUCK!
JEFF KEANE IN
COMING SOON
The FOX AND THE HOUNDS
LOOKS OVER COMING ATTRACTIONS.
REST ROOMS
LADIES
MEN
OOPS!
RUNS HAND DRYER THROUGH 5 CYCLES.
EXIT
GETS DRINK OF WATER.
ASKS DOORMAN THE TIME.
SEES OLD NEWS-PAPER-- READS THE COMICS.
NOTHING SELLS FOR A DIME. REMEMBERS THE MOVIE.
POP CORN
BOUNCES ON LOUNGE.
LEARNS ALL ABOUT BEING A CASHIER.
FINDS A DIME!
LISTENS IN ON PHONE CONVERSATION.
SPOTS FRIENDS. TELLS THEM MOVIE'S PLOT SO FAR.
SPACE ATTACK
CHECKS OUTSIDE WEATHER.
PRICES CANDY, ICE CREAM, POPCORN, ETC.
LOOKS IN COIN RETURN FOR CHANGE.

YEEULK! THAT'S MUSHY!
DOES THAT MEAN YOU AND MOMMY ARE IN LOVE, DADDY?
CAREFUL, MOMMY--YOU'RE SQUASHING THE FLOWERS DADDY BROUGHT YOU.
KNOW WHAT IT LOOKS LIKE TO ME? THE ENDING OF ONE OF THOSE REAL OLD MOVIES.
I'M GONNA TELL GRANDMA!
BARFY'S BARKING AT YOU, DADDY--HE THINKS YOU'RE HURTING MOMMY.
SHOULD WE GO TO OUR ROOMS AND LET YOU ALONE, MOMMY?
I SEE PEOPLE DO THAT ALL THE TIME ON DAYTIME TELEVISION.
AND ALL WE GET IS A LITTLE PECK ON THE CHEEK.
WHEN'S DINNER, MOMMY?
PJ WANTS TO BE NEXT.
HOW CAN YOU KISS THAT LONG WITHOUT LAUGHING?
BIL KEANE

NO, BILLY, YOU CANNOT GO DOWNTOWN ALONE. YOU'RE MUCH TOO YOUNG FOR THAT.
FEET OFF THE CHAIR! YOU'RE OLD ENOUGH TO KNOW BETTER!

OKAY--
HOP
IN.
I CAN'T
HOP THAT
HIGH,
DADDY.
WELL,
JUST
CLIMB
IN!
BIL
KEANE

DO I HAFTA EAT ANY MORE OF THIS MOMMY?
I'M FULL!
I'M DONE.
CAN I BE EXCUSED, DADDY?
MMM! I'M HUNGRY! I'LL HAVE THE STEAK, FRENCH FRIES, AND SOUP, AND...
$
I WANT THE GIANT CHEESEBURGER, A DOUBLE SHAKE...
FRIED SHRIMP, RICE, CORN ON THE COB, AND...
Menu
BIL KEANE

SUNDAY PAPER
THEY MAKE IT BIGGER ON SUNDAY BECAUSE DADDY HAS MORE TIME.
THAT'S NOT HOW CHARLIE BROWN SOUNDS ON TV.
COMICS
REAL ESTATE
GORGEOUS home for large family on 5 wooded acres. Fireplace, den, family rm. 4 br, 3 baths, mod. kitch., conv. to schools, shopping,
SOMEBODY'S IN THE CELLAR AND DADDY DOESN'T LIKE IT.
SPORTS
WHY DO YOU HAVE THIS PAPER OVER YOUR HEAD?
BIL KEANE

TODAY WE'RE GOING TO THE ZOO TO SEE ALL THE ANIMALS!
PJ
BIL KEANE

# Christmas Is Coming
By Billy

PJ Telling Santa what He wants

..not a creature was... not a creature was...

Stirring!

Christmas ~~Pajent~~ ~~Pagint~~ Play

Bringing Home the Tree

Mommy and Daddy talking

Writing to Santa Claus

Jeffy Trying to Sleep at Night

WE HAVE TO GET DADDY'S PRESENT!
SOME-THING HE'LL REALLY LIKE!
WILL YOU HELP US PICK IT OUT, MOMMY?
MEN'S
Gifts
TOYS and

JAN.
MARCH
MAY
SEPT.
NOV.
DEC.

BIL KEANE
DADDY, AFTER YOU GLUE DOLLY'S HOUSE CAN YOU FIX MY TRUCK?
ONLY 364 SHOPPIN' DAYS TILL CHRISTMAS!
I'M GLAD SANTA DIDN'T BRING US MANY CLOTHES. GRANDMA BRINGS THOSE.
THE CANDY IN OUR STOCKINGS LOOKS LIKE SOME OF THE TRICK OR TREAT STUFF FROM HALLOWEEN.
SEEMS LIKE WE'RE HAVIN' TWO SUNDAYS IN A ROW!
ARE WE GONNA HAVE ANOTHER CHRISTMAS DINNER TODAY, MOMMY?
HOW MANY DAYS TILL MY BIRTHDAY?
IS IT OKAY TO MAKE A LIST OF THE THINGS SANTA FORGOT TO BRING?
WHAT'S HAPPENED TO ALL THE CHRISTMAS MUSIC ON THE RADIO?
PJ'S TOUCHING MY TOYS!
THE NEEDLES ARE FALLING OFF THE TREE ALREADY.
BILLY
DOLLY
BAKE SET
WHY DID SANTA PILE ALL THOSE EMPTY BOXES OUT BACK?

I WANT TO GROW UP TO MAKE SOME FAMILY HAPPY.
CHRISTMAS TREES
THAT'S A GOOD ONE, DADDY!
IT'S THE PRETTIEST EVER!
EVERYBODY STAND AROUND THE TREE.
BIL KEANE

YOU BETTER HURRY UP, DADDY-- IT'S STARTING TO SNOW AGAIN!
I WISH MOMMY COULD FIND MY BUCKET AND SHOVEL FROM THE BEACH SO I COULD HELP YOU.
IF YOU DIG UP A SLED, DADDY, IT'S MINE. I LEFT IT OUT HERE BY MISTAKE.
GRANDMA SAYS THERE ARE NO TWO SNOW-FLAKES ALIKE-- I'M GOING TO CATCH A COUPLE AND SEE IF SHE'S RIGHT..
ARE WE JUST DOIN' OURS OR ARE WE GONNA DO ALL THE HOUSES ON THE STREET?
COULD YOU STOP FOR AWHILE AND BUILD US A SNOWMAN?
WHY DOES IT LOOK LIKE WE'RE ALL SMOKING?
WE HAVE TO STAY OUT HERE FOR AT LEAST A HALF HOUR 'CAUSE MOMMY SAID SO WHEN SHE WAS DRESSING US.
ARE YOU DIGGING THIS PATH SO YOU'LL HAVE SOME PLACE TO JOG?
WATCH OUT, PJ! YOU MIGHT GET SHOVELED.

# Does "The Family Circus" have an unlimited source of new cartoon ideas?

With a crew of models like this how could any cartoonist be short of fresh material? Max, Jesse, Jason and Claire Keane make sure their Granddad isn't short of love either.